Kids Like Me in China

Kids Like Me in China

KIDS LIKE ME
IN CHINA

by

Ying Ying Fry

with
Amy Klatzkin

Photographs by
Brian Boyd, Terry M. Fry and Ying Ying Fry

YEONG & YEONG BOOK COMPANY
St. Paul, Minnesota

Yeong & Yeong Book Company
1368 Michelle Drive
St. Paul, Minnesota 55123-1459
www.YeongandYeong.com

Designed by Mark Ong

Printed in Hong Kong by C&C Offset

First Edition

10   9   8   7   6   5   4   3   2   1

Publisher's Cataloging-in-Publication
(Provided by Quality Books, Inc.)
Fry, Ying Ying.
  Kids like me in China / by Ying Ying Fry with Amy
Klatzkin ; photographs by Brian Boyd, Terry M. Fry and
Ying Ying Fry. — 1st ed.
  p.   cm.
  ISBN: 0-9638472-6-0

  1. Orphanages—China—Changsha (Hunan Sheng)
2. Orphanages—China—Changsha (Hunan Sheng)—Pictorial
works. 3. Fry, Ying Ying—Journeys—China—Changsha
(Hunan Sheng) 4. Changsha (Hunan Sheng, China)—
Description and travel. I. Klatzkin, Amy. II. Boyd,
Brian, 1950- III. Fry, Terry M. IV. Title.

HV1320.C43F79 2001   362.7'32'0951'215
                    QBI01-200810

Proceeds from the sale of this book benefit the Foundation for Chinese Orphanages and
the Amity Foundation.

To Li Yongqing

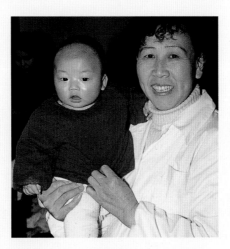

Hi! My name is Ying Ying.

I am eight years old, and I live in San Francisco. Like lots of kids in my city, I'm Chinese American. But I wasn't born that way. When I was really small, I was just Chinese. Then my American parents came and adopted me, and that's how I got the American part.

There are lots of kids like me who were born in China and adopted by parents from other parts of the world—not just the United States but Canada and Europe and Australia too. Wherever we go, we often meet families like ours.

When kids adopted from China grow up in other countries, they usually don't look like their parents. But sometimes they do. You can't always tell by looking.

I don't look like my parents, so everybody knows I'm adopted. Sometimes I think about it a lot, and sometimes I'm way too busy with other things, like school and soccer and homework and piano practice.

When I'm by myself, I like to read about things that happened a long time ago, like baby Moses floating in a basket down the river, or Hua Mulan fighting to save China, or Anne Frank writing her diary. Sometimes I think about what happened to *me* a long time ago. That's hard, because I can't remember being born. I can't remember being a baby. But there are some things I know.

I was born in a province of China called Hunan. I don't know who my birth parents are, and I don't know for sure why they could not raise me. But I do know this: When I was a tiny baby, my birth parents made a really big decision. Because they couldn't be my forever family, they decided to take me someplace where I would be safe and someone would take care of me.

A policeman found me outside a police station and brought me to the orphanage in Changsha, the capital city of Hunan. There a caregiver named Li Yongqing made me warm and safe and loved me until my forever family came to adopt me. I know this because she told me. But I don't remember any of it.

I used to be scared of the word *orphanage*. It felt dark and spooky. But then, when I was five, I got to visit four orphanages in China. The babies were cute, and the children looked a lot like me. Their caregivers looked like some of my teachers. They sang and laughed, and I liked them.

After that I really wanted to go see *my* orphanage. What is it like to be a baby there? Do the little kids play? Do they celebrate birthdays? Do the big kids go to school? Do they have to take math tests?

I had to wait a few years, but finally, last December, my parents took me to see my orphanage and the city where I lived as a tiny baby. I was really excited and also a little scared. Would I like it there? Would the people there like me? Most of all, I wanted to see my caregiver. I wanted to see someone who knew me and loved me when I lived in China.

I stayed with my parents in a hotel near the orphanage. The very first day we walked over to visit. On the wall outside, big red characters say, "Changsha is my home." Can you believe it? Did someone write that for me?

We took a picture at the orphanage gate. Actually, it's not just an orphanage. Old people also live there, and there's a hospital too. So it's called a Social Welfare Institution. I looked up all those words. *Social* means it's for people. *Welfare* means giving people things they need to do well. *Institution* means it's a public place, like a school, not private, like a family.

I wanted to see the babies first. In my orphanage, babies and toddlers live together on the eighth floor of a new building. When I was a baby I lived in an old building, but that

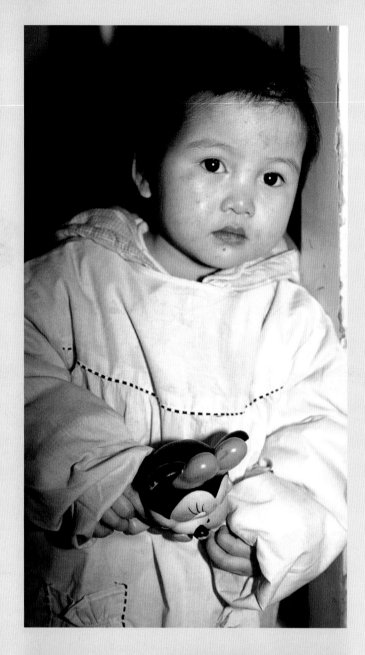
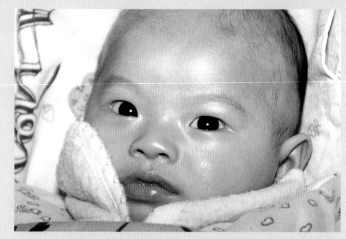
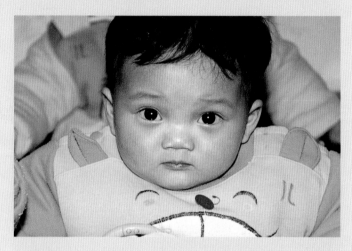
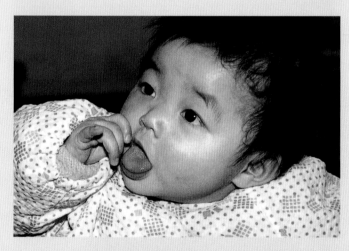
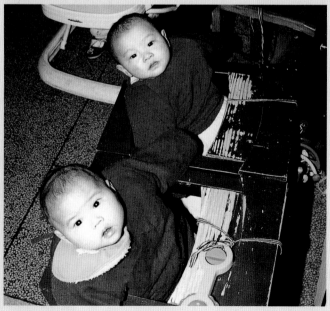
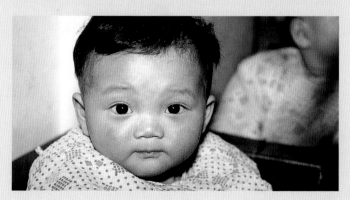

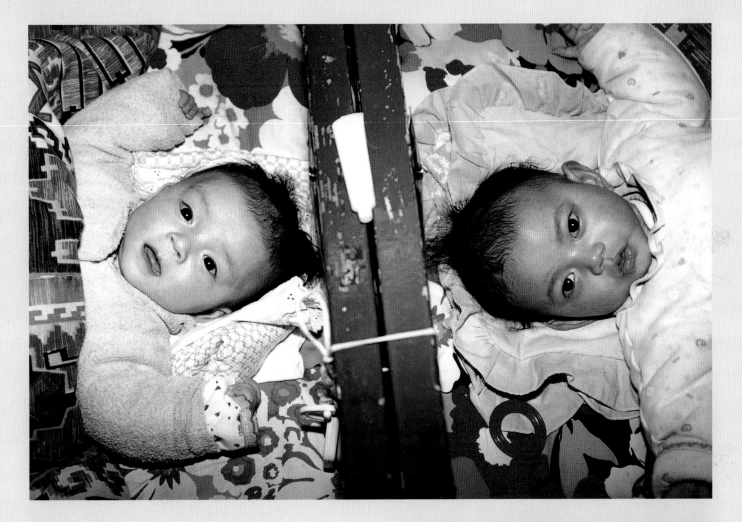

building was torn down. All over China old buildings are coming down and new ones are going up. It's not just orphanages that are changing.

There were a whole lot of babies on the baby floor when I visited—more than 100! Some were just a few days old. Most were a few months old, like I was when I lived there. Two little babies sleep in each crib, one head at one end and one at the other. In winter the babies are bundled up in warm clothes under thick covers. Most of them sleep with their hands up by their heads. I still sleep like that! Some babies sleep in old green cribs like I did, but most have brand new cribs, and they all have new sheets and comforters. They have new clothes too.

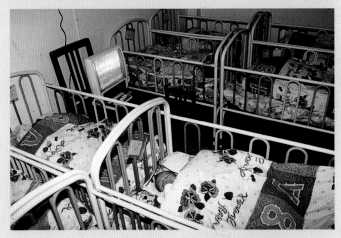

Many parents who have adopted from China give money to buy things for the children who are still waiting for families. The babies at Changsha have some nice things now—toys and tape players, heaters to stay warm in winter and air conditioners to cool off in summer. I helped the orphanage buy a

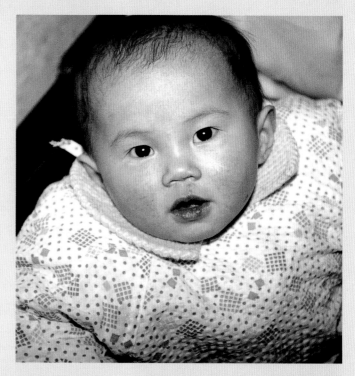

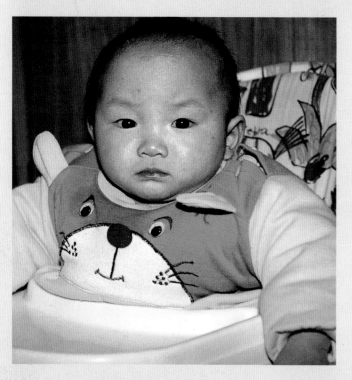

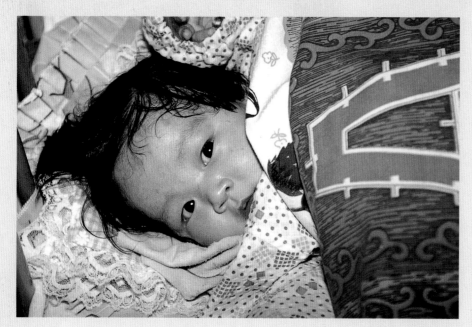

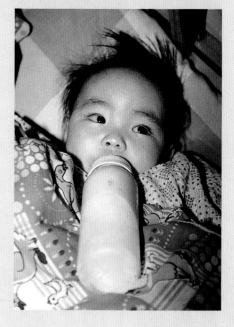

heater by sharing some of my allowance. I'm proud that I can help.

This is my caregiver! I call her Li Ayi, which means Auntie Li. She carried me and fed me when I lived at the orphanage. She smiles and laughs a lot. At first I had to listen hard to understand her because she speaks Mandarin with a Hunan accent. The Mandarin teachers at my school in San Francisco come from other parts of China where people pronounce things differently. When Li Ayi speaks Changsha dialect to the other Ayis, I can't understand at all. I learned just one word: *gamma*. That means frog. In Mandarin we say *qingwa* for frog, so you see they're not at all alike.

Li Ayi was so happy to see me! She calls me Ying Ying, but when she talked to the other Ayis she used my orphanage name, Zhou Sheng. The Ayis all came over to meet me. I

heard one ask, "She's one of *ours?*" Some wanted to touch me and ask me questions. I liked it, and I also felt shy because I didn't know them yet.

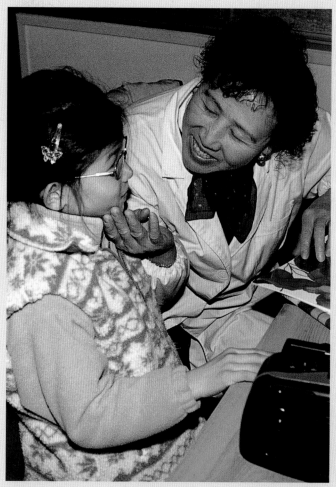

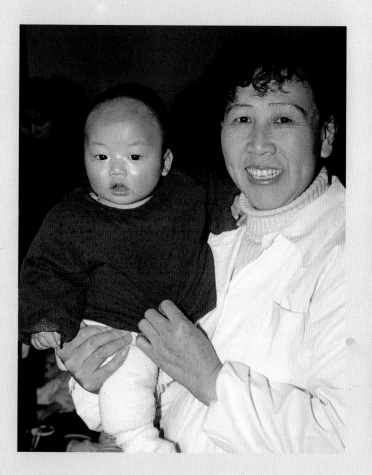

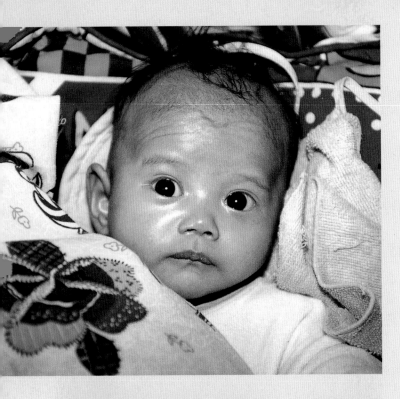

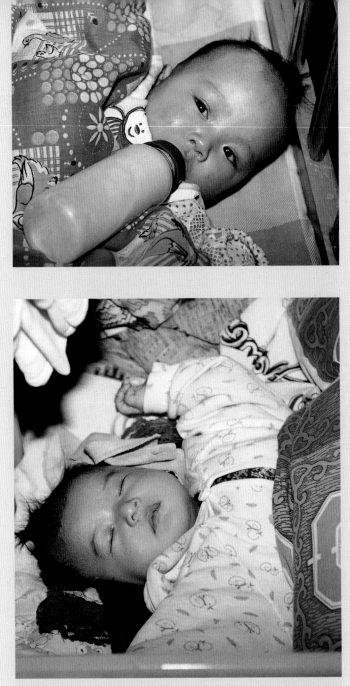

I went to see the babies every day for two weeks. I helped give them bottles. I got to hold them and tickle them. I liked to make them smile.

There are so many babies to feed and take care of. The Ayis are always busy. If they tried to pick up just one baby to feed her, lots of other babies would cry because they are hungry too. So the Ayis give all the babies their bottles at once. The little babies don't know how to hold their own bottles, so the Ayis use the babies' quilts as holders. I got good at picking up bottles that fell out of babies' mouths, and I let the Ayis know when a bottle was empty. The Ayis said I was very helpful.

When the little babies finish their bottles, they usually fall asleep. Except if they are wet. Then they cry. Babies cry a lot. They sleep a lot too. But they don't play much. I guess when I lived in the orphanage I cried and slept a lot too.

The big babies are a lot more fun than the tiny ones. They can't talk yet, but they know how to play. They could tell I was a kid like them, and they liked to watch me do things.

Those babies look chubbier than they really are because they have so many clothes on. Even with heaters, the air inside is cool. People in China wear lots of layers in winter. At the orphanage I wore four layers on top, but just one pair of pants. Changsha people wear two layers on their legs in winter, but I could not get used to that.

Those babies sure look cute sitting around

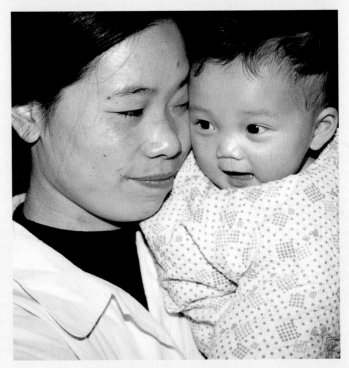

the heater, like they are having a meeting. Others scoot around in walkers. Music plays on a tape recorder, and they all like that. Sometimes an Ayi sings to them. They play with toys and with each other. Sometimes two of them try to play with the same toy, and one of them will cry. When I saw that happen, I'd give them both a toy, and they'd stop fussing.

While the babies play and fuss and scoot, the Ayis are very busy. They hold babies, wipe noses, clip fingernails and sing songs. Then they fold clean diapers or make up the cribs or get fresh clothes ready.

A little while after their bottles, all the

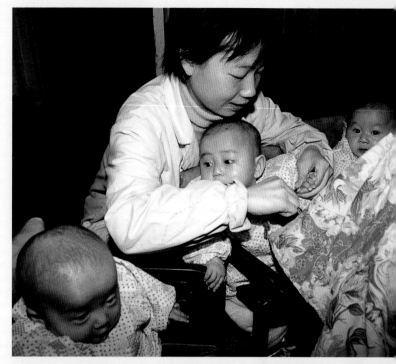

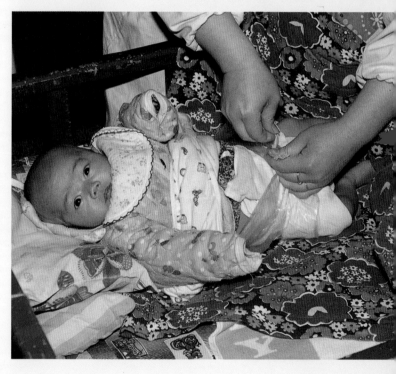

babies need changing. The Ayis change them one at a time. After they take off a dirty diaper, they carry each baby over to a big tank of warm water to wash her bottom. When the baby is clean and dry, she gets a fresh diaper and sits down to play again or goes back in her crib. Then the Ayis pick up another baby.

I don't think the Ayis ever stop working. They hardly ever sit down. They even eat lunch standing up.

Every day a doctor comes to check the babies. Sometimes, if they need medicine, they get it right in the head! Li Ayi says that helps the medicine work quickly. A few days later, the baby with the topknot was all better.

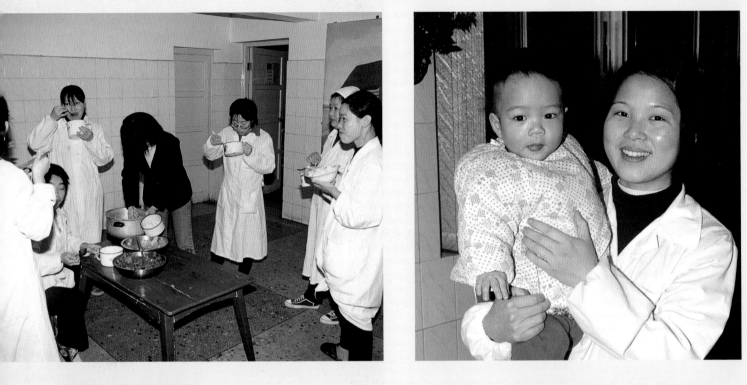

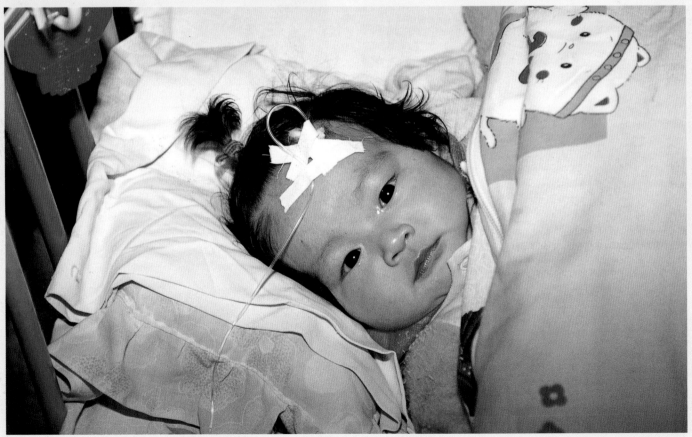

My favorite place on the baby floor is the playroom. Big babies and toddlers get to play there every morning and afternoon. The playroom has lots of windows and piles of toys. There's a tape player for music and a new wooden floor. Grownups take off their shoes in the playroom, but we kids don't have to.

Some of the toddlers can talk, and they called me *jiejie,* "big sister." They got to know me and wanted me to play with them. They're big enough to eat real food like rice and vegetables, and I got to help feed them back in their room.

I hope all the orphanage children get families soon. Some will probably get families in China. Some will get families in other countries. I think they will be happier when they have forever families of their own.

I know why there are so many babies in Chinese orphanages. The government of China is worried that there are too many people. They are afraid there won't be enough food or homes or jobs for everybody if the population keeps growing. They put up billboards and write big characters on walls telling people that they'll be happier and better off if they have just one child. You can see those signs in every city in China.

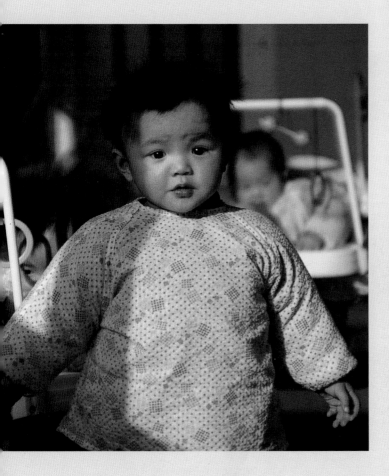

To get people to have small families, the government made some rules, and they're really strict about them. Parents don't get to choose how many children they have. Usually they're allowed to have only one if they live in the city, one or two if they live in the countryside. If they're caught having more, the government can make them pay huge fines and might also take away their jobs or their house, or force them to get an operation that makes it impossible to have another baby. Many parents are afraid of big punishments like that. And that's why a lot of babies end up in orphanages in China.

But the babies didn't do anything wrong! Why do they have to lose their first families? I don't think those rules are fair to babies.

Then there's the girl thing. Most of the babies on the baby floor are girls like me. There are only a few boys. You can't tell from their clothes or their hair, but you can tell when their diapers are changed.

I think I know why most of them are girls. But it's not easy to explain, because in China people love boys *and* girls. I know because I've met lots of parents and grandparents there who have girls and love them very much.

But in China it's a boy's job to take care of his parents when they're really old and can't

work anymore. Girls are supposed to take care of their husband's parents.

And there's one more thing. When boys in China grow up and get married, they pass on their family name to their kids. The family name is like a last name, only in Chinese it comes first. I don't understand why the family name is so important, but I guess for some people it really, really is.

Because boys pass on the family name to their children and take care of their parents when they're old, some people in China feel that they *have* to have a boy. Especially if they live in the countryside and don't have a lot of money to save for the future. They might be happy if the first baby is a girl, but if they have more kids than they're allowed to have, and *all* of them are girls, then they worry a lot about how they will live when they are old.

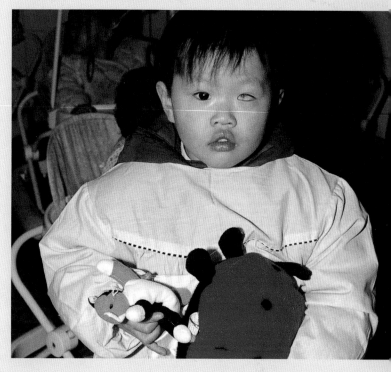

Sometimes they decide they can't raise another baby girl, no matter how much they love her, because they need to try again for a boy.

And then they take that new baby girl someplace safe, where she will be found quickly and taken care of and maybe get a new family—in China or some other country—who can love her and keep her forever.

Maybe that's what happened to me. I don't know for sure.

Maybe I have a sister in China somewhere. Maybe I have a brother. I wish I knew. I hope one day I'll find out.

I wish I knew what my birth mother looks like. Does her face look like mine?

Sometimes I think a lot about stuff like that. But I don't talk about it much.

Sometimes I looked at all those babies in all those cribs and I didn't know what to think. Sometimes I just had to leave the room.

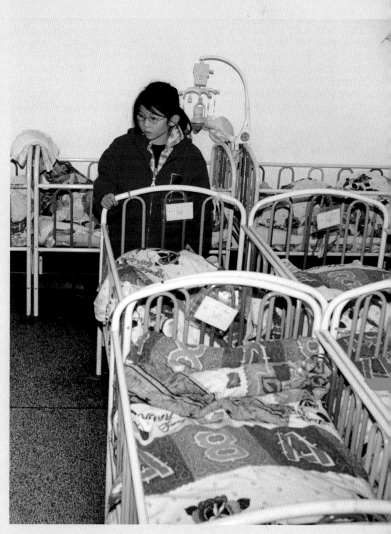

The baby floor is just one part of the big social welfare institution. I got to meet kids in other parts too. Most of these children have special needs, and there are just as many boys as girls. Maybe their birth parents didn't know how to take care of them or didn't have enough money to pay for doctors and that's how they ended up in the orphanage.

I used to think "disabled" meant blind or deaf or using a wheelchair, and there are children like that at the orphanage. Others have a problem with their mouth or their foot or something else that doctors can fix. Some of these children will be adopted. Others will grow up at the orphanage and get a job and take care of themselves when they're older.

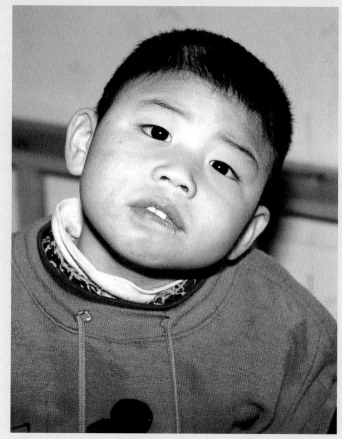

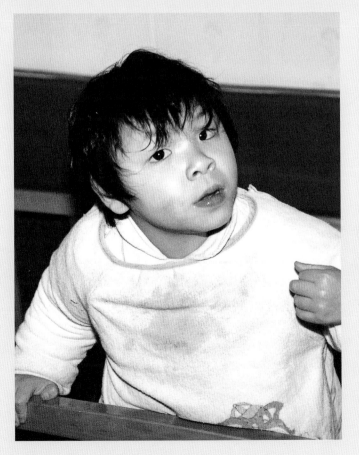

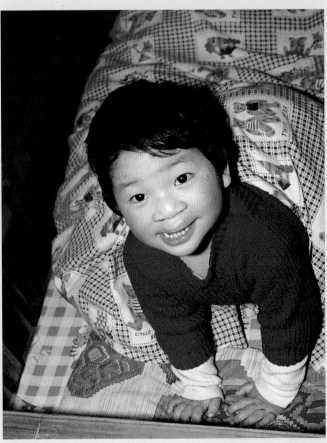

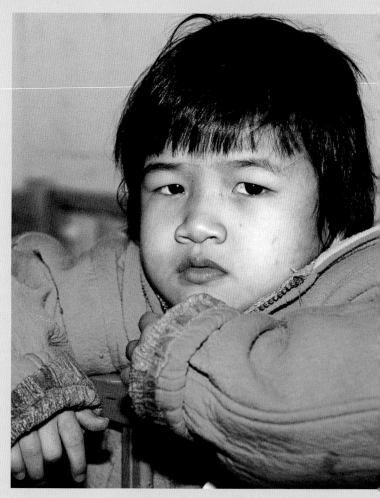

But a lot of the disabled children at the orphanage were born with really big problems. They need lots of special care. When they grow up, they will still need help to do ordinary things. Children like this live in every country in the world, sometimes in a family and sometimes in an institution. I didn't know that before.

The Ayis said these children are special. Their lives are different from mine, but they're just as important.

Some of the kids at my orphanage are even older than I am. I saw them mostly on weekends, because during the week they go to school in the city. They are growing up at the orphanage, and they are my friends.

On the big kids' floor, there are just as many boys as girls. They each have their own bed, with two or three beds in a room. The girls' rooms are in one group. The boys live next

door. They each have a backpack for school, and they've decorated the walls to make the rooms look nice. The big kids don't have many things, but they take really good care of what they have.

I think they take good care of each other too. They're like a big family, except there's no mom or dad. Two grownups live with them and help look after them, but that's not the same as having parents. Those kids have to do a lot for themselves.

When they met me, they were surprised to hear that I'd lived at the orphanage too when I was a baby. "You're one of *us?*" one girl asked. I felt shy speaking Chinese to them, but they didn't mind when I made mistakes. They were really nice to me.

I liked to play with the girls, especially the ones close to my age. Li Hong is nine and a little shorter than me. Wang Zhao is even shorter, and she's ten. She likes lipstick. Xiao Wang is ten too. He likes to wear a baseball cap.

Zhou Min is eleven. She loved our video camera. So did the other kids. They shot a lot of bumpy video inside the big kids' rooms.

Sometimes when my parents were in another part of the orphanage, I'd go to my friends' rooms to play. It was different without my parents there. I talked more, and the kids asked me more questions: "Do you like America? Do you like China? Do you like your parents?" Yes, yes, yes.

Most mornings the big kids leave the orphanage at seven to go to school. They stop to have noodles for breakfast on the way. Like lots of kids in China, they come home for lunch and take a rest in the middle of the day. Then they go back to school until late afternoon. They showed me their homework. It's not that different from mine. They have math

tests too, but they only do a little bit of English.

Sometimes I met the big kids on their way back from school, and we went down the street to buy snacks. The orphanage kids do a lot of things together.

When I visited them on Sundays, I also got to see Yang Lan. She's twenty-seven years old, and she's been at the orphanage since she was six. Now she works there as the laundress, looks after the older girls, and does some modeling in her spare time. There's a beautiful picture of her on the wall by her bed.

Yang Lan talks with her hands because she is deaf. The other kids helped her share her

story. She remembers coming to the orphanage. She cried and cried for weeks. But after a while she made such good friends, they were like sisters and brothers. Then, when she had grown up, her aunt sent her a letter about her birth family. They live far away in another province. Now she visits them every year at Spring Festival, but the orphanage is still her home.

Yang Lan said we have a lot in common. We both lost our first parents, and we both started our new lives at the orphanage. She says it's

important for everyone to make the best of their lives. She has made a good life for herself, and she wants me to have a good life too.

I think about my friends at the orphanage a lot. It's sad that they don't live in a family. I would miss mine very much. But still, I sometimes wonder what it would be like to grow up at the orphanage with them.

When I wasn't at the orphanage, I got to see a lot of the city and some of the countryside nearby. They are like two different worlds.

The people we met in the city live in apartments and work in shops or offices or schools or factories. But in the countryside, where most Chinese people live, families usually build houses near the fields where they work. Some houses are old-fashioned, with just one floor and a courtyard. If families have enough money, they build new white houses with two or three floors and big windows. In China, old and new are often side by side.

It's exciting to explore a Chinese city. I loved the courtyards and gardens of Yuelu Academy, which is more than 1,000 years old. And I liked the Pinghe Department Store too, which is bigger than Nordstrom's and much more crowded.

Even ordinary things can be different. When I went to a beauty parlor to get my hair cut,

they gave me a head massage with the shampoo. It felt great.

Restaurants in Changsha serve really spicy Hunan food. I'm getting used to chili peppers, but I like the noodles and breads you can buy on the street even better.

When the weather's nice, there are parks and playgrounds to play in. They have merry-go-rounds and Ferris wheels and bumper cars, just like amusement parks at home. But they also have bridges and pavilions that look really Chinese. And the kids who play there all look Chinese too. I fit right in.

I met kids everywhere we went. Except for a few twins, they were all only children, without brothers or sisters. In the countryside we saw bigger families, but not in the city.

My friend Chuqi is an only child, and so am I. Chuqi is a year younger than me, and he lives with his parents in a new apartment in Changsha.

On weekends, when he's not studying, he likes to watch videos and play games. He taught me how to play *weiqi*, a really old Chinese board game.

Chuqi's life is a lot like mine, but not exactly the same. His mom takes him to school early in the morning and picks him up at the end of the day. But not in a car or bus. He rides on the back of her motorcycle! At lunchtime he eats at school, and at night he has lots of homework. He's even learning English. But right now, if we want to talk to each other, we have to speak Chinese.

When I'm with Chuqi's parents and aunts and uncle, I look like part of the family.

School is a big part of my life at home, so I really wanted to see a school in China. My wish came true when a young teacher named Millie invited us to a Christmas party at Mayuanwan Primary School.

When we arrived, all the children came out onto the blacktop for morning exercises to music. At my school we never do that. We just run around and play tetherball at recess.

A lot of kids came to the party afterwards in Millie's classroom. She teaches English to fourth, fifth and sixth graders, and each class has around 40 students—twice as many as my class at home. The children sang a welcome song, and then Millie introduced us. "This is Ying Ying," she said, "and these are her parents. Ying Ying was born in Changsha, and now she lives in America." She didn't say anything about adoption. She just treated us like a regular family.

Many of the children had brought cards and gifts for me. Some of them had made beautiful paintings and calligraphy and papercuts. I even got to wear a red scarf like a regular Chinese schoolgirl.

After the gifts it was time for performances. Some kids sang. Some played music. Some danced. Nobody seemed embarrassed. At my school, most kids are shy about performing in front of each other, but the kids at Mayuan-wan Primary School looked like they really enjoyed it.

In Millie's class the students all use English names, like Lucy and Angel and William. That's kind of like my Chinese class at home, where everybody uses Chinese names even if they're not Chinese. Millie says that English names are fashionable among young people in Chinese cities these days.

A boy called Johnson was the last to perform. He didn't dance to Chinese music or play Western classical music like the other children. Instead, he pretended to be the American rock star Michael Jackson singing "Beat It." He danced and played air guitar and shook hands with everyone just like singers on MTV. Then he got down on one knee and handed me a rose! He was really funny.

For the rest of the morning we played games. I tied for first place in musical chairs, but the other games were harder, especially the chopsticks race. To play, put a bunch of marbles in a bowl of water. Then you and some

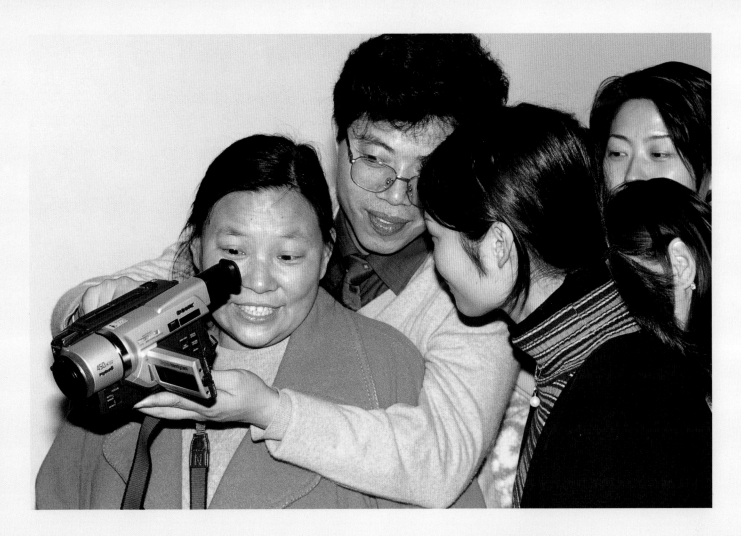

friends use chopsticks to pick up the marbles and put them in a dry bowl. Whoever moves the most marbles in two minutes wins. Try it!

At the end of the morning we took class pictures and said good-bye. Some of us went to Johnson's apartment for lunch. While his parents watched the performance on video, we played games on their laptop. My dad has the same computer. Johnson's mom has a home office like my mom's. Our families may live far apart, but we have a lot in common.

A few days later I met Millie and some of her students at a fast food restaurant in the city. One of the girls is my pen pal now. I hope I can go to their school again some day. I kind of feel like I belong.

Back at our hotel room, I decorated the walls and windows with the cards and gifts from Millie's students. It was the end of December and time to go home. I missed my friends, and I needed to get back to *my* school. But part of me wanted to stay a little longer in China.

China isn't my home anymore, but it's where I was born. Even though that was a long time ago, it's a really important part of my life. If I hadn't been born in China, I wouldn't be me.

And there's one more thing: It's good to know there are so many kids like me there.

題目：我喜歡中國　二年綠班：備丁鶯

希望可以再去中國

想去長城走很久

再去兒院看小朋友

可以去看長江

可以去長沙看工

可以去北京看天安門

I LIKE CHINA

I hope I can go back to China.
I'd like to go to the Great Wall and walk a
　　long time,
Go back to my orphanage and see the little
　　children.

I could go to Wuhan and see the Yangzi River.
I could go to Changsha and see my friend
　　Lucy.
I could go to Beijing and see Tian'anmen.

Acknowledgments

All books are collaborations, this one more than most. The text was constructed from Ying Ying's journal and from audiotapes, videotapes and interviews with her. The opinions, observations and questions are all hers, and she exercised final approval over the wording. The explanation of the likely origins of most babies in Chinese orphanages is her retelling of the pioneering research of Kay Johnson, Wang Liyao and Huang Banghan. Other children adopted from China helped too: LiLi Johnson contributed to the discussion on origins, and Yang West and Meili Isaacson shared stories from visits to their orphanages.

In China, we are deeply grateful to Director Zhou Hongyi and his dedicated staff at the Changsha First Social Welfare Institution. Special thanks go to Yang Lan and the *xuesheng ban*—the schoolchildren at the orphanage who embraced Ying Ying as one of their own. We also thank the Hunan Province Bureau of Civil Affairs and the Hunan Provincial Adoption Service Center for supporting adoptive families. Thanks too to International China Concern, which cares for 100 disabled children in Changsha. The headmistress, teachers (especially Millie Wang) and students of Mayuanwan Primary School dazzled us with their kindness and talent. Chuqi's and Johnson's families opened their hearts and homes to us, and Mark Ma and Christine Xue devoted countless hours to our welfare. Those who supported us in China merit our deepest gratitude, but we alone are responsible for any errors, omissions or inaccuracies in the book.

In the United States, we thank Deann Borshay Liem, Jane Brown, Susan Caughman, Walton Chang, Sara Dorow, Elizabeth J. Klatzkin, Qin Song Ng, Mark Ong, George Tapper, Jie Wang and Kan Zhao for their invaluable insights and support.

Finally, we thank Wu Anan of the Amity Foundation, the Orphanage Assistance Programs of FCC–New York and the Foundation for Chinese Orphanages for supporting children in Changsha and dozens of other welfare institutions in China.

A WEB PAGE FOR KIDS

Share your story about kids like *you* in China! Children who have gone back to China are invited to submit their words and pictures for a special children's section of the Yeong and Yeong website (www.YeongandYeong.com). Send submissions by email to BBoyd@YeongandYeong.com. To protect children's privacy, only first names, ages, and state, province or country will be listed.